Messiah REVEALED

in the SABBATH

by

Hannah Nesher

VOICE for
Israel

ISBN# 978-0-9733892-5-8

For speaking engagements please contact Hannah:

Hannah Nesher, Voice for Israel
Suite #313- 11215 Jasper Ave.
Edmonton, Alberta
T5K 0L5 Canada

www.voiceforisrael.net

Cover design by James Vanderwekken - jvnderwe@hotmail.com

DEDICATION

To the God of my fathers, Avraham, Yitzchak and Yaacov,

יהוה

אהיה אשר אהיה

To You whose name says

You will be whoever You will be –

Thanks for being all I have ever needed!

And to Your Son and Messiah Y'shuah

ישוע

For your obedience to the Father

For being led like a lamb to the slaughter

For pouring out your soul unto death

So that I could live!

A Special Thank You

I would like to say *todah rabah* (thanks very much) and publicly acknowledge my debt of gratitude towards some of the many people who helped with this work.

First of all, to my mother and father who gave me life. Thank you for your courage in training up this daughter of yours through all our ups and downs. Although we may not always agree on theology, your love has remained constant.

To David, for applying your excellent technical skills to help bring this book to publication. Thank you for your love, encouragment and steadfast faith - and for the gift of our two wonderful children.

To my children, Clayton, Courtney, Timothy, Liat, and Avi-ad, who each supplied material and inspiration for my writing. Thanks for your patience with the crazy times in our family - for loving and forgiving me. Big hugs to Clayton for his great technical support.

To our ministry partners for your faithful love, fervent prayers and generous support. May you be fully rewarded by the God of Israel under whose wings you have taken refuge - Ruth 2:12

To James Vanderwekken for his awesome graphic design work and technical support. You are a treasure!

To Denis Vanderwekken & his late wife, Corrie for their friendship, support, and help in the journey. Corrie - I miss you!
To Marilyn for your intercession & willingness to proofread.

Most of all, to the Holy Spirit (Ruach Hakodesh), for giving me the inspiration, motivation, and words to write.

Todah rabah! (thanks so much!) תודה רבה

CONTENTS

CHAPTER ONE

WHAT IS SHABBAT?

Shabbat, the Sabbath, is the first of the "Feasts of the Lord", as described in the 23rd chapter of the book of Leviticus (Vayikrah)." In Hebrew, the word used is a mo'ed מועד (or moadim מועדים in the plural form). This is the word that God uses to describe the appointed times when we are to hold special meetings. They are not so much 'feasts' or 'festivals' (although they may include these); but are more of a divinely appointed time to meet and celebrate or remember important aspects of our walk with God – past, present, and future. In the beginning (Genesis/B'reisheet), God institutes Shabbat, a Sabbath day of rest for all of humanity. It stands as a memorial of God's creation of the universe.

> **"Thus the heavens and the earth, and all the host of them, were finished. And on the seventh day God ended His work which He had done, and He rested on the seventh day from all His work which He had done. Then God blessed the seventh day and sanctified it, because in it He rested from all His work which God had created and made."**
> (Gen 2:1-3)

In essence, God placed a boundary on His role as Creator of the Universe. He modeled a truth for us and that is: after working and creating and manipulating our universe, causing things to happen in our world for six days straight, we need to say, by faith, 'it is finished, complete and done'. Now I am just going to rest from all my labors and efforts. Often, we need to say this by faith, since nothing around us seems to have been brought to completion. Unlike God, we are limited beings and sometimes never seem to accomplish all we would like to in any designated week. But with all the piles of unfinished business, we can, in obedience to the model God showed us, say 'dayeinu' (It is enough) – I have worked enough now for a human being and I will now stop and rest. People are, by our very sin nature, boundary pushers if not outright boundary breakers. Like little children, we're always trying to push the limits of grace. But the fear of the Lord is the beginning of wisdom.

A Foundational Feast of the Lord

Shabbat is often not thought of as a feast of the Lord, but in actuality it is the foundational feast upon which all the others are built. What happens if we fail to build a solid foundation for our home? When the storms and floods come, that house will likely fall, not being able to withstand the additional strain. In the same way, when we do not build our lives upon the foundation of God's cycle of time for humanity; when we instead operate according to our pace of time, then when extra pressure or stress comes upon us through trials and tribulations, we may not be able to stand. For this reason, God has given us Shabbat, a day of Sabbath rest.

All of our activity must come out of a place of rest and peace. This concept goes all the way back to the Garden of Eden.

God created the first man and woman on the sixth day and on the seventh day, He rested. Adam's first day on earth after his creation was a day of rest! Doesn't it seem logical that in all of his excitement, Adam would want to explore this wonderful garden, set some short term and long term goals written and then immediately get started on his ten point action plan? But no - being comes before doing. The commandment to rest on the seventh day is still one of the Ten Commandments, one that we disregard at our own peril. In Hebrew, the word for Sabbath is Shabbat שַׁבָּת which is related to the word 'la'shevet' לָשֶׁבֶת – to sit. Here is a beautiful gift from God – the right to just sit and do nothing and not feel guilty about it but rather to feel holy in all of our sitting! Wow! Great news for couch potatoes; but let's not forget the other six days we are supposed to be working. ☺

Many people these days are suffering from fatigue, stress and chronic, widespread pain in their bodies as well as an emptiness of soul and despair of spirit. I have also experienced these afflictions. I kept hearing Yeshua say, *"Come to me, you (insert your own name) who are weary, worn out, and heavy burdened, and I will give you rest."* And I would answer, *"Well, I'd love to, Lord, but you see, I have these little kids and a husband and a ministry and have so very much to do! So as soon as I get through this endless to do list, I will rest, O.K.?"* Again and again, in a still, quiet voice, the Holy Spirit spoke to me, **"In returning and rest you shall be saved; in quietness and confidence/trust shall be your strength (might or courage.)"** (Isa. 30:15) But just like the Israelites refused *"No, for we will flee on horses"*, I also resisted God's gracious offer,. **"Therefore the Lord will wait, that He may be gracious to you"**

The Lord knows how to wait so much better than we do. I wonder how many precious, weary, worn out saints are riding fast horses while the Lord is patiently waiting for them to slow down so that He may reveal to them His grace? I am often amazed at how extraordinarily patient God is in dealing with our foibles, but also how doggedly persistent He is in His attempts to lead us to healing and wholeness. In our microwave oriented society, we look for a quick fix. *"Nuke it, God, we cry. We have places to go, people to see, things to do."* But God showed me that He not only wanted to heal my body physically, but to bring 'wholeness', which in Hebrew is the word, 'shalem', שלם - a derivative of 'shalom', שלום meaning peace.[1] Because our physical selves are so intricately connected to our emotional, spiritual and mental states, my healing would only come once I learned to obey Him, not only in what He wanted me to *do* for Him, but also in what He wanted me to *not do*. We can come to think that we are what we do; but this is not the truth of who we are. It is through Yeshua's offering of his own life that we are made whole, complete, and perfect – shalem - שלם **"For by one offering He has perfected (השלים) forever those who are being sanctified** (made holy/ kadosh).**"** (Heb. 10:14)

We are becoming so caught up in all the frantic activity of our lives with the constant information overload through the internet and e-mail – our inboxes are overflowing to the max so we just set up more and more accounts to try and handle the load. People send forwards and we just can't resist one little peek – this one is so cute, or so beautiful or so profound. And before we know it, more time has passed than we can afford. Children sit in front of the TV or computer or play videogames while mothers play catch up, though it seems more like the chasing after the carrot that can never be really apprehended than a job well done. It used to be that life flowed in the rhythms of grace;

---

1 For a more complete word study, see 'Shalom, Shalom Jerusalem' in the articles archives of our website or in our first Hebrew course, Shalom Morah: www.voiceforisrael.com

but these days it seems like I must often choose between several different scheduled events that all take place at the same time. Most of these are good things, but we just can't do it all! I see mothers absolutely frazzled, just trying to keep up with all their kids' lessons and appointments and activities. The other day, my youngest son asked if he could play with another boy from his class. His mother was standing right there, so I asked her and after several minutes of listening to her describe their frantic and complex schedule for the next few days, I was sorry I even asked. And this is kindergarten!! My heart goes out to people whose lives pass them by in a blur like this. I know because I've been there – still am at times, although I have determined by God's grace to carve out His designated 'time-out' space in my life on the seventh day of each week called Shabbat. It is meant to be a twenty-four hour period of rest, and renewal of mind, body and spirit.

Wayne Muller, in his book, *'Sabbath: Remembering the Sacred Rhythm of Rest and Delight'* [2] explains it in this way:

> "Because we do not rest, we lose our way. We
> miss the compass points that show us where to
> go, the quiet that gives us wisdom."

A Relief From Our Busyness

In a tension-filled, competitive, hurry-up world, Shabbat is an island of time, a sanctuary to create for ourselves and our families. The sun will still rise if we stay away from the malls and shut off the phone for a day and rest. It is necessary for the survival of our souls, especially in these end times, to isolate ourselves from all the pressures of life and rest in the arms of our heavenly Father.

---

2 Batmam Books, N.Y. 1999

Wayne Muller states,

> *"Life is what's happening while you're too busy to notice...In the relentless busyness of modern life, we have lost the rhythm between action and rest...there is a universal refrain: "I am so busy." We say this to one another as if our exhaustion were a trophy, our ability to withstand stress a mark of character. The busier we are, the more important we seem to ourselves and, we imagine, to others. To be unavailable to friends and family, to be unable to find time for the sunset (or to even know the sun has set) to whiz through obligations without time for a single mindful breath – this has become the model of a successful life."Yet the more our life speeds up, the more we feel weary, overwhelmed, lost. Our life and work rarely feel light, pleasant or healing. Instead, as it all piles endlessly upon itself, the whole experience of being alive begins to melt into one enormous obligation."* [3]

Are any of you nodding your heads in recognition of the feelings Muller describes? Why is this happening to us? Because we have forgotten God's Shabbat. Often, it's all I can do to make it to Yom Shishi (the sixth day), with all the demands of work and family obligations, trying to be everything to everyone and then some; But knowing that soon Shabbat will arrive and I can rest makes all the difference in the world. With all our many

---

3   Wayne Muller, '*Sabbath: Remembering the Sacred Rhythm of Rest and Delight*', (Random House, 2775 Matheson Blvd. E. Missisauga, Ont. L4W 4P7, Canada)

responsibilities, we can feel terribly guilty when we simply do nothing but rest. Shabbat gives us this guilt-free liberating permission to stop and restore our souls – to just 'be'. Shabbat, however, is more than just permission – it is a commandment from the Creator of the heavens and the earth. The Creator of our minds, souls, and bodies wrote an owner's manual, the Bible, and we would do well to heed its instructions.

A Day of Rest

"There remains therefore a rest to the people of God." (Heb. 4:9)

Many Christians say 'Jesus is my rest', as if this eliminates any need for us to rest physically from our work. Yes, Shabbat points to the future state of perfect rest and peace in the Messianic Age, and yes, we have spiritual peace and rest in Yeshua, but we still need a period of physical rest and renewal. Shabbat is a break from the routine of work. It gives us a rhythm and cycle to our sense of time. Here in Israel, each day is measured by its relationship to the Sabbath. As the week progresses, preparations are made to receive the Sabbath bride. On Yom Shishi (the sixth day), most women are busy finishing the housework, shopping for last minute provisions, preparing the traditional braided bread called challah, and cooking a special Sabbath meal. By the afternoon, men are off work, construction ceases, buses stop running, businesses close their doors after the frantic pre-Shabbat rush. Peace begins to descend upon the pale yellow stones of Jerusalem as the sun sets. Candles are lit and the family gathers for a special meal, to praise God, to welcome this holy day, and to bless our children. We wake up to the quiet of streets with little traffic and a glorious day ahead of knowing that we need do nothing other than spend time with one another and with our God, reading and discussing His scripture reading for the Sabbath, and catching up on our rest.

Many people seem to carry a negative perception of the Sabbath, as if it is a day set apart to curb our freedom and restrict our activities, like some sort of cosmic killjoy. Most people, unless they have inherited a rather large fortune of money, engage in meaningful (or not quite so meaningful) work to provide for their daily needs. Many people enjoy their work, but to others, it is just a job they endure to make a living. Even so, how would you feel if your boss brought you into his or her office and gave you the day off – with pay - told you to go home, rest, take it easy, not to worry about anything! Would you go home and mope and curse your bad luck for having to take a day off? Would you protest to the boss that you really don't need a day off, and if He makes you take a day off, then He is forcing you to commit the horrendous sin of legalism?!

Shabbat occurs every seven days, since our Creator knew that this interval of rest would be necessary to ensure that work does not rule our lives. We are so caught up in 'doing' that it can become our whole identity. "What do you do?" is usually one of the first questions we ask people when wanting to get to know them. We sing, "Lord, I want to be used by You", and we seek for what we may do or accomplish for Him, but often He is more concerned with simply who we are becoming. Shabbat gives us time to reflect on the priorities in our lives, and to focus more on the spiritual than the physical.

In the New Testament, Martha was so caught up in preparing for Yeshua's visit that she could not slow down long enough to enjoy His presence. She was utterly annoyed with Mary, who simply sat at His feet. But Yeshua rebuked Martha and told her not to be so worried about all these trivial matters; that Mary had chosen the better way. Of course we need to work and are commanded to be diligent and warned against laziness. The command is to work six days and rest one. Shabbat gives us that day we need to simply be Mary and sit at His feet. Some spouses and children feel neglected by the incessant demands of 'work' upon their loved ones. Shabbat ensures that we give sufficient love and attention to those in our families who need our undivided time.

The question may be asked, "Do we need to rest if we do not feel tired?" We are to pattern our rest after God who rested. Do we think that the God who created the universe was tired and needed a rest after six days of hard work? Of course not! The Bible says,

> **"Have you not known? Have you not heard? The everlasting God, the LORD, the Creator of the ends of the earth, neither faints nor is weary. His understanding is unsearchable."** (Is. 40:28)

God did not rest because he was exhausted. Even creating a universe is not hard for God. But God rested in a different sense – he stopped creating. We rest in a Sabbath sense, when we stop creating, stop interfering with our world. For six days, God demonstrated His mastery over the universe by actively changing it, but on the seventh day, He rested. So, too, do we rest when we relinquish our mastery over the world. That is why, although many activities may be restful, they are creative pursuits, or involve changing something in our world and are therefore not keeping the Sabbath. This is why the Word of God tells us not to go after our own pleasures on this holy day. It is not simply to be a day of rest and recreation, but a day of ceasing our striving, our creative efforts.

God never intended for Shabbat to become a legalistic, joyless, dutiful conformity to a set of do's and don'ts (mostly don'ts). It is God's gift to humanity, a gift that sets us free from the bondage of believing the lies that we have to do it all; and that the source of our value and worth is in our works. Can resting be holy? God's word says that it can be, when done His way.

> **"The appointed times of the Lord, which you shall proclaim to be holy convocations, these are My appointed times. Six days shall work be done, but the seventh day is a Sabbath of solemn rest, a holy convocation. You shall do not work on it; it is the Sabbath of the Lord in all your dwellings."**
> (Lev. 23:2-3)

Shabbat: The Universal Equalizer

We need to keep in mind that these are not the Feasts of the Jews, nor are they the Feasts of Israel, but they are God's feasts. God says "they are MY appointed times." If we are people who belong to the Lord, then they belong to us as well; they are part of our inheritance – Jew or Gentile. Many non-Jewish people of God are beginning to discover these 'moadim' and to celebrate them as God commanded. I rejoice to see churches holding Passover Seders and building communal sukkot (booths) for the Feast of Tabernacles. What a testimony to the Jewish people that Christians worship the same God and keep His commandments! These are not 'Jewish' holidays (or holy days) as most people consider them. Although this command was spoken to the children of Israel, all the holy people of God may receive the privilege of celebrating the Lord's feasts on His holy days. Gentiles who were once aliens from the commonwealth of Israel, strangers from the covenants of promise, without hope and without God in the world have now been brought near through the blood of the Messiah, Yeshua.

> **"...That at that time you were without the Messiah, being aliens from the commonwealth of Israel and strangers from the covenants of promise, having no hope and without God in the world. But now in Messiah Yeshua you who once were far away have been brought near by the blood of Messiah."**
> (Eph. 2:12-13)

This means that Gentiles have obtained citizenship in the commonwealth of Israel and a place in the covenant of promise through the Messiah. When one becomes a citizen of a new country, don't they need to pledge their allegiance to uphold the laws of the land? Can one be a citizen of a nation and break the government's laws? And so, like Ruth, Gentiles who are grafted into the olive tree need to pledge their allegiance to the people of Israel and to our God and His commandments.

Shabbat, or the Sabbath, is the first of God's feasts that He commands us to observe. What a privilege that together, the wild olive shoots that have been grafted in and the natural branches may both share in the same nourishing sap of the root and fatness of the olive tree.

> **"And if some of the branches were broken off, and you, being a wild olive tree, were grafted in among them, and with them became a partaker of the root and fatness of the olive tree, do not boast against the branches. But if you do boast, remember that**

you do not support the root, but the root supports you." (Rom. 11:17-18)

Shabbat (Sabbath rest) has remained a crucial aspect of Jewish identity as a people set apart, sanctified, and holy unto God. In fact, the expression used to indicate that a Jewish person is Orthodox (or Torah-observant) is that they are '*Shomrei Shabbos*', which means that they keep Shabbat. Therefore, many people consider the seventh day Sabbath as something belonging exclusively to the Jewish people; but God created the Sabbath in the beginning of time (Breisheet/Genesis) before the first Jew ever walked the face of the earth.

Many Christians, who accept the validity of the Ten Commandments, seem to forget that the law of the Sabbath is most comprehensively stated in the fourth of the Ten Commandments:

> **"Remember the Sabbath day, to keep it holy. Six days shalt thou labour, and do all thy work: but the seventh day is the Sabbath of the Lord thy God: in it thou shalt not do any work, thou, nor thy son, nor thy daughter, thy manservant, nor thy maidservant, nor thy cattle, nor the stranger that is within thy gates: for in six days the Lord made heaven and earth, the sea, and all that in them is, and rested the seventh day: wherefore the Lord blessed the Sabbath day, and hallowed it."**
> (Ex. 20:8-11)

Notice that even the cows and the slaves enjoy a day of rest. Some Jewish people employ what they call a 'Shabbat goy', a Gentile who will perform some of the many tasks that they, under strict rabbinical law, are forbidden to do: things like turning off or on a light, but this is not really work. To my disappointment, while living in the Negev of Israel, I saw the Thai workers going to labor in the hot greenhouses on Shabbat as usual. Such things should never be in God's holy land. Even our servants are to take this day off to rest and relax. Shabbat is a testimony to God's love for all people and His desire that all be treated humanely and fairly. It was not just the Jewish people who were to rest on Shabbat, but also the aliens and strangers, the servants and slaves. On this day, everyone stands equal before the Lord in deserving a day of rest – slave and free, Jew and Gentile, male and female, rich and poor.

Shabbat is a gift from God to us with a promise of great blessings to those of us who will receive. Even foreigners who bind themselves to the Lord to keep His Sabbaths and not desecrate them will receive joy in the Lord's house of prayer on His holy mountain.

> **"Also the sons of the foreigner who join themselves to the Lord, to serve Him, and to love the name of the Lord, to be His servants – everyone who keeps from defiling the Sabbath, and holds fast My covenant – even them I will bring to My holy mountain, and make them joyful in My house of prayer. Their burnt offerings and their sacrifices will be accepted on My altar; for My house shall be called a house of prayer for all nations."** (Is. 56:6-7)

Many Christians use the seventh day, Saturday, as a busy day of shopping and housecleaning and errands. Sunday is stressful as well, with morning and evening church services, and numerous ministries that they are committed to and involved in. They really have no day designated as a day to simply rest! What have we done with this fourth of the Ten Commandments? Chisel it out of the rock each week? If even the animals and slaves are to be given this day to rest, how much more so must God desire to see His people receiving and accepting the gift He has given us to rest on Shabbat.

The scriptures state that salvation was to come to the Gentiles to provoke the Jews to jealousy. Before I began honoring Shabbat as a day of rest, however, I was instead jealous of my Jewish relatives who took the seventh day to sleep in, stay home, and rest. We were not given the option to choose any day of the week as the Sabbath, like "eenie meenie, willy nilly, I choose Monday." The Sabbath is not merely one-seventh part of the week, but designated specifically by our God as the seventh day.

> **"...The seventh day is the Sabbath of the Lord thy God..."** (Ex. 20:10)

Because the biblical day begins at the evening dusk and last until the next evening, Sabbath is observed from Friday sundown to Saturday sundown. (Lev. 23:32) All God's creatures are to rest on the seventh day just as our Creator set for an example to us.

> **"Six days you shall do your work, and on the seventh day you shall rest."** (Ex. 23:12)

A Memorial of Our Freedom "Avadim Hayinu"

At the Feast of Passover, we retell the account of our deliverance from Egypt and sing a song called, '*Avadim Hayinu*', meaning, "*We were once slaves*". The song concludes, "*But now we are sons of freedom*". When we labored as slaves in Egypt we did not have the liberty of rest, but because of God's great love and mercy, He rescued us from our affliction and oppression and set us free to serve Him.

> **"He brought out His people with joy, His chosen ones with gladness...That they might observe His statutes and keep His laws."** (Ps. 105:43, 45)

God heard the groanings of the children of Israel whom the Egyptians kept in bondage, and He remembered His covenant with them. And so He brought the people of Israel out from under the burdens of the Egyptians, He rescued them from their bondage and redeemed them with an outstretched arm and with great judgments. He took this people to be His very own and promised to be their God. (Ex. 6: 5-7)

Shabbat is, therefore, a memorial of God's rescue of Israel from slavery in Egypt under Pharaoh. As Believers, when celebrating Shabbat each week, we can remember God's individual rescue of each one of us from the kingdom of darkness. Through God's son, Yeshua HaMashiach (the Messiah) we may enter into the Kingdom of Light and find divine forgiveness.

> **"He has delivered us from the power of darkness and conveyed us into the kingdom of the Son of His love, in whom we have redemption through His blood, the forgiveness of sins."** (Col. 1:13-14)

Each Shabbat, we may celebrate His goodness to us in delivering us from serving the 'Pharaoh of this world', Satan, and from the bondage of sin. Many Christians mistakenly believe that 'Jesus set them free from the law'. In fact, this is a grave misunderstanding of what Yeshua's sacrifice accomplished for us. Yeshua clearly states that He did not come to abolish the Torah (law).

> **"Do not think that I came to destroy the Law or the
> Prophets, I did not come to destroy, but to fulfill."**
> (Matt. 5:17)

What does Yeshua Himself tell us about the many people
who teach that we are not 'under the law'?

> **"Whoever therefore breaks one of the least of these
> commandments and teaches men so, shall be called
> least in the kingdom of heaven, but whoever does
> and teaches them, he shall be called great in the
> kingdom of heaven."** (Matt. 5:19)

I don't know about you, but I certainly would rather be called
great in the kingdom of heaven than the least! The liberty we have
won in the Messiah is not freedom from God's commandments,
the Torah (law), but from sin itself. Sin need no longer be our
cruel taskmaster.

> **"For sin shall not have dominion over you, for you
> are not under law but under grace."** (Rom. 6:14)

Yes, we are under grace, but does this give us license to
sin?

> **"What then? Shall we sin because we are not under
> law but under grace? Certainly not!"** (Rom. 6:15)

And what is sin but lawlessness! We have been set free from
sin to become slaves to righteousness.

> **"And having been set free from sin, you became
> slaves of righteousness."** (Rom. 6:18)

Before we received Yeshua as our Saviour, we were free to sin, but what fruit did this bring us of which we are not ashamed? In the end these things bring death and destruction.

> **"What fruit did you have then in the things of which you are now ashamed? For the end of those things is death."** (Rom. 6: 21)

God did not set His people free from slavery in Egypt just so they could go their own merry way. No, He brought them out of Egypt in order to take them to Mount Sinai and give them His Torah. He rescued His people so that they could serve Him and live as a holy people.

> **"But now having been set free from sin, and having become slaves for God, you have your fruit to holiness, and the end, everlasting life."** (Rom. 6:22)

In fact, the Word tells us that without holiness, no one will see God.

> **"Pursue peace with all people, and holiness, without which no one will see the Lord."** (Heb. 12:14)

Once we walked in the flesh, our carnal minds hostile to God's laws, but now Yeshua has set us free to walk in the Spirit and obedience! Halleluyah!

> **"Because the carnal mind is enmity against God; for it is not subject to the law of God, nor indeed can be. So then, those who are in the flesh cannot please God. But you are not in the flesh but in the Spirit, if indeed the Spirit of God dwells in**

**you. Now if anyone does not have the spirit of the
Messiah, he is not His."** (Rom. 8:7-9)

Each Shabbat we can remember to thank God that we are
no longer slaves, but sons and daughters of freedom. We are not
forced to work seven days a week, but have this one day a week,
Shabbat, to rest. We are not compelled to obey Satan to sin, but
free to obey God's commands. Therefore, the Sabbath is not only
a day of physical rest, but also a day of holiness.

"Remember the Sabbath day to keep it holy."
(Ex. 20:8)

A Sign of Our Betrothal

The seventh day Sabbath is also the central sign of the
covenant between God and His people. The Hebrew word for
this 'sign' is 'ot' אות.

**"Moreover also I gave them My Sabbaths, to be a
sign אות between Me and them, that they might
know that I am the Lord that sanctifies them."**
(Ezek. 20:12)

The covenant relationship between God and His people could
be considered a type of betrothal, as in a marriage. The Lord said
He would go to prepare a place for us, and that He would return
for us, and take us to this place that He has prepared for His
bride. This is a picture of ancient Jewish betrothal and wedding
customs. The betrothal is sealed with a benediction over the cup
of wine. The betrothal, in ancient times, could only be broken
with a divorce. Yosef (Joseph) was betrothed to Miriam (Mary),

although they had not yet had intimate relations and did not dwell together. Those being prepared to be the 'Bride of Christ' are betrothed to the Messiah Yeshua through the New Covenant, but the marriage, the consummation, the 'dwelling together' has not yet taken place. One day, the Bride and her Bridegroom will dwell together.

> **"...Behold, the tabernacle of God is with men and He will dwell with them, and they shall be His people. God Himself will be with them and be their God. And God will wipe away every tear from their eyes; there shall be no more death, nor sorrow, nor crying. There shall be no more pain, for the former things have passed away."**
> (Rev. 21:3-4)

The bridegroom then goes away for a period of time (which the father determines) to prepare a place for his bride. She doesn't know when he will return, but must keep herself ready, just as we must prepare ourselves for the time of Yeshua's return for us.

> **"Let us be glad and rejoice and give Him glory, for the marriage of the Lamb has come, and His wife has made herself ready."** (Rev. 19:7)

One day, the bridegroom returns with his groomsmen, carrying torches and singing songs of joy, to retrieve his bride and take her to the home he has prepared for her. One day, Yeshua, who has returned to the Father to prepare a place for His bride, will return for her.

> **"Let not your heart be troubled; you believe in God, believe also in Me. "In my Father's house**

**are many mansions; if it were not so, I would have
told you. I go to prepare a place for you. "And if I
go and prepare a place for you, I will come again
and receive you to Myself; that where I am, there
you may be also."** (John 14:1-3)

Usually, the sign of a betrothal in today's society is an
engagement ring. Even if the couple disagrees on an issue, or
argues, or experiences a rift in their relationship, as long as the
bride-to-be keeps wearing the engagement ring, we can know
that the betrothal is still intact and all will be well. However, if
the woman throws the ring back in her intended husband's face
and says, "Here, take it, I don't want it!" we can surmise that the
covenant is in grave danger and may even be broken.

The seventh day Sabbath is the sign given by God to His
people of their covenant relationship. What is He to think if His
people throw it back in His face? Or what if the man gives the
woman a beautiful engagement ring and she takes it to a jeweler
and asks for the ring to be melted down into a different form,
more to her liking? Isn't this what many people have done when
God has given us the seventh day as a Sabbath rest, and instead,
people choose Sunday, or any other day?

The Chuppah

The great and historic event that took place between God and
Israel at Mount Sinai may be likened to a marriage ceremony.
This took place, according to Jewish tradition, at Shavuot (Feast
of Weeks or Pentecost). The conditions of the covenant were
laid out; the responsibilities of each party clearly specified.

In a Jewish wedding ceremony, these are written in the

ketubah, the marriage contract. It states what the husband is responsible for in the marriage and also the wife, as well as what each may expect from the other. God clearly states at Mt. Sinai, His expectations of His bride, and what He is prepared to offer. Israel, His bride, said, "I do"

> **"And all the people answered together, and said, 'All that the Lord has spoken we will do.'"** (Ex. 19:8)

Every bride is given a ring, a token, a sign that she is betrothed. What is the sign of betrothal God gave to Israel? It is the Shabbat. God said it will be a 'sign' between Him and the people of Israel; it is the wedding ring. Many Christians mistakenly believe that God has 'divorced' Israel as His bride. But God says of his bride, *"Where is her get?"* (Is. 50:1) The 'get' is a Jewish divorce document, without which a Jewish woman would never be able to remarry under strict Orthodox Jewish law. It is always given on the initiative of the husband, not the wife. If the husband refuses to give the 'get', then the woman is abandoned without hope of re-marriage. My own sister spent years in rabbinical courts trying to coerce her ex-husband into handing over her 'get'. Finally he gave in, but if he hadn't, her current marriage (civilly legal) would have been considered adulterous by Jewish law and her children from this union illegitimate. The 'get' is an extremely important document for Jewish women. Without it, they are still 'legally' bound to their husband (in a spiritual sense).

God did not give Israel her 'get', even though she betrayed him through spiritual adultery. Like Hosea, God remained faithful to His faithless wife, always hoping for her return and restoration. One Christian author stated that God already 'left one bride at the altar'. But this is false. God's covenant with Abraham and his descendants through Isaac and Israel (Jacob) is as unbreakable as his covenant with heaven above and the earth below.

> **"Thus says the Lord: 'If heaven above can be measured, and the foundations of the earth searched out beneath, I will also cast off all the seed of Israel for all that they have done, says the Lord.'"**
> (Jer. 31:37)

God is a covenant keeping, not a covenant breaking God.

> **"My covenant I will not break..."** (Ps. 89:34)

I believe that the bridegroom also gave to His bride a wedding gift. This is the land of Israel, given as a promise to this special nation. Can we consider the rage of the bridegroom towards those who attempt to take away His beloved's wedding gift?

Other Covenants – Other Signs

God has given to His people other signs of His covenants. A covenant is called in Hebrew 'brit' אות. When He made a covenant with mankind that He would never again destroy the earth with a flood, He gave us the sign (ot) {אות} of the rainbow in the sky as a reminder.

> **"...This is the sign (ot) אות of the covenant (brit) ברית which I make between Me and you, and every living creature that is with you, for perpetual generations. I set My rainbow in the cloud, and it shall be for the sign of the covenant between Me and the earth."** (Gen. 9:12-13)

Similarly, when God made a perpetual covenant with Abraham and his seed for the land of Israel, He gave him a sign אות - the circumcision of all male children on the eighth day.

> **"And you shall be circumcised in the flesh of your foreskins, and it shall be a sign אות of the covenant between Me and you."** (Gen. 17:11)

When God adopted the people of Israel as His very own and became their personal God, He gave them another sign: Shabbat.

> **"hallow My Sabbaths, and they will be a sign אות between Me and you, that you may know that I am the LORD your God."** (Ezek. 20:20)

What then, about those who are followers of Yeshua the Messiah, who is the mediator of a New Covenant? Does this sign of the covenant given to the people of Israel through Moses still apply to New Covenant Believers? The prophet Jeremiah prophesied about a future time when God would make a New Covenant with His people.

> **"Behold the days are coming, says the Lord, when I will make a new covenant with the house of Israel and with the house of Judah..."** (Jer. 31:31)

What happens to God's law (Torah commandments) under this New Covenant? Jeremiah states this clearly – it becomes an internal way of being, rather than an external ritual. It becomes written in our minds and our hearts to keep God's commandments.

> **"I will put My law (Torah) in their minds, and
> write it on their hearts; and I will be their God,
> and they shall be My people."** (Jer. 31:33)

This, then, is the sign of the New Covenant – not freedom
from the law as so many consider, but the opposite – obedience!
This is the sign that the Spirit of God lives in us – that we are
compelled from within to keep God's commandments.

> **"I will put my Spirit within you and cause you
> to walk in My statutes, and you will keep My
> judgments and do them."** (Ezek. 36:27)

If the people of God believe they are keeping God's
commandments by refraining from alcohol, dancing, or gambling,
which are man-made laws while breaking God's divine laws then
they are sadly mistaken and will have to answer to the judge who
may well ask them why they did not read His book! Anyone who
does not keep Shabbat as a day of rest and a holy day is keeping
only nine of the Ten Commandments. God has created this world
based on a set of laws; our lives work and we are blessed to the
extent that we follow these laws. For example, because of the
law of gravity, if I jump off a tall building, I will fall and probably
injure myself, perhaps fatally. Ignorance of this law does not
protect me from the consequences of breaking it. Because I know
about the law of gravity, I choose not to jump off tall buildings or
out of airplanes without a parachute. This is my choice. I could
choose to disregard the law and suffer the consequences. God
gives us this choice. He promises to bless us to the extent that we
obey His laws and commandments and to curse us to the extent
that we break them. He sets before us life or death, blessings or
cursing, but then ends with, 'choose life'. Just like King Darius
could not negate his own law that he had instituted which threw

Daniel in the lion's den and King Ahashverosh could not negate his own law that he had instituted giving people permission to kill the Jews on the 13th of the month of Adar, the King of Kings and Lord of Lords will not negate His own laws. God does not take pleasure in the death of the wicked; He does not want even one human soul to perish. But He gives us the choice to obey His commandments or to break them and we must live with the consequences. He is not a co-dependent enabler that allows us to get away with all our hurtful, self-destructive and sinful behavior. He allows us to feel the sting of the sin in our lives. It is the same way with our decision to keep Shabbat as a holy day of rest or not. If we don't do it intentionally, it will never happen, for the world has other plans for us.

I realize that very few Christian leaders would agree with what I am telling you about the Sabbath. This is not a situation that only occurs today; it happened in ancient times as well that the religious leaders of the day did not teach people to keep the Sabbath. Because of this, God was profaned. We must obey God rather than man when the two contradict.

> **"Her priests have violated my law and profaned My holy things; they have not distinguished between the holy and unholy, nor have they made known the difference between the unclean and the clean; and they have hidden their eyes from My Sabbaths so that I am profaned among them."** (Ezek. 22:26)

A Double Portion

On Shabbat we enjoy the freedom from providing for our material needs. In refraining from work, or doing anything to provide for our needs on this day, we prove our trust in a God who provides. Just as the Israelites were instructed to gather a double portion of manna on the sixth day, and not to gather on the seventh, we are demonstrating our trust in God that He is a loving Father and provider and we are free from fear and anxiety.

> **"Therefore do not worry, saying, 'What shall we eat?' or 'What shall we drink?' or 'What shall we wear?' For after all these things the Gentiles seek. For your heavenly Father knows that you need all these things. But seek first the kingdom of God and His righteousness, and all these things shall be added to you."** (Matt. 6:31-33)

Many people suffer from fear of lack, especially those who grew up in families where finances were in short supply or where the people in their family of origin worried about money. Unfortunately, this very fear of lack blocks our prosperity rather than the abundance we desire. By resting on Shabbat and consciously refusing to worry about or do anything related to our vocation, we free ourselves from bondage to this fear or worry. We acknowledge God as YHVH Yir'eh, our provider. If we are working diligently, faithfully tithing and giving generous offerings, blessing Israel, especially the household of faith, giving to the poor and obeying God's commandments to the best of our abilities (including Shabbat), living in peace and unity with others, then we should have no fear or even concern for our material concerns. God is a good father and He withholds no good thing from those who seek Him. In our family, we try not to talk or even think about the worldly or secular concerns of our lives on this day. We try not to discuss financial matters, business, or everyday concerns on Shabbat. We try to keep our eyes on the Lord and even confront one another if we begin to treat the Sabbath as 'just an ordinary day' in our actions, or speech.

Does God take this sign of our trust seriously? We can look at the Bible account of the Israelites as an example. God sent manna from heaven each day, which the people were to go out and gather for their daily portion. If they gathered for the next day, whether out of fear or greed, it would turn into worms. But on Yom Shishi (the sixth day), God gave the Israelites a double portion in order to provide for Shabbat that they would not have to gather on this holy day.

> **"Six days you shall gather it, but on the seventh day, the Sabbath, there will be none."** (Ex. 16:26)

He did this,

> **"...In order that I may test them, whether they will walk in My law (Torah) or not."** (Ex. 16:4)

Is it not possible that whether we keep the Sabbath day or not is God's test of our love and devotion to Him? 1 John 5:3 states,

> **"For this is the love of God, that we keep His commandments. And His commandments are not burdensome."**

Here in Israel, the people have a unique way of distributing second hand goods – they leave unwanted items beside the big

garbage bins. This is a sign that it is up for grabs and the first one
to take it keeps it. It's like an unofficial Salvation Army system.
Often, beautiful and expensive items are left by the garbage, by
those who are moving or just want to give them away. When we
arrived in Israel, we came with nothing except two suitcases each
and had to find a way to furnish an entire apartment. That this was
accomplished was a true testimony to the miraculous provision
of a generous God. But we often saw a valuable item out beside
the garbage on Shabbat. We were tempted to go out and bring it
inside, fearing that someone would haul it away sometime during
the day. But the fear of God, which is the beginning of wisdom,
kept us from going out to gather on Shabbat. And the item of
our desire was always still there at sundown. God honored our
obedience and saved it for us.

What happened to the one who dared break this commandment
to keep Shabbat?

> **"Some of the people went out on the seventh day
> to gather, but they found none. And God said
> to Moses, 'How long do you refuse to keep My
> commandments and my laws? See! For the Lord
> has given you the Sabbath...'"**   (Ex. 16:27-29)

The Lord could be shouting the same question to us today.
'How long…?' Indeed, how long will the people of God refuse to
keep God's commandments? The penalty for breaking Shabbat
was death. The man who dared to gather wood on Shabbat was
stoned to death by the entire community upon God's command.
God is serious about this commandment. Just as serious as the
commandment, "Thou shalt not murder". And yet many people
of God consider this as merely a trivial suggestion.

A Day to Stay Home

The people were commanded to stay in their homes for Shabbat and not to go out. And so they stayed home and rested. Many people consider Shabbat a day of recreation and use it as a 'family fun day'. So they pack up the kids and the car and the dog and the diaper bag and pack a lunch and blankets, and half the household, and set off for a day at the park or beach and by the time they get there all are exhausted and cranky. And when they get home, Mom and Dad have to unload the car, dump all the sand and dirt out of the clothes, put everything away. NOW they're really ready for a Shabbat rest. But it's too late. It was spent on recreation. Been there, done that, got the T-shirt. This is not Shabbat. God warns us not to use this day for our own pleasure or recreation, and promises great reward for our obedience. Those who keep the Lord's day honorable and call the Sabbath a delight; those who don't do as they please and don't confuse recreation with rest and holiness will find their joy in the Lord and will ride on the heights of the land and feast on their inheritance.

> **"If you turn away your foot from the Sabbath, from doing your pleasure on My holy day, and call the Sabbath a delight, the holy day of the Lord honorable, and shall honor Him, not doing your own ways, nor finding your own pleasure, nor speaking your own words, then you shall delight yourself in the Lord; and I will cause you to ride on the high hills of the earth, and feed you with the heritage of Jacob your father. The mouth of the Lord has spoken."** (Is. 58:13-14)

I have a story to relate about my own personal struggle with

this issue. One of my hobbies is scrapbooking. I love to cut
and glue and paste all my kids' pictures, photos and memories.
Someone introduced me to it and now I'm hooked. I love making
special albums for people, like for my parents' 50th wedding
anniversary or my Mom's 65th birthday. I also created a heritage
album with photos and the story of our family history, going way
back to the Pioneer days. I don't know why I love it so much
but I do; it seem to satisfy a creative urge within me; perhaps I
regress in time to my kindergarten days which seem simpler than
the life I now live. For whatever reason, I love scrapbooking!
The problem has been that for the last decade or so, I have been
so immersed in childrearing and working and 'ministry' related
activities that I have not devoted time to this hobby. So when I
saw an ad in the paper advertising a whole weekend of 'scrap till
you drop', my heart yearned to go. When my husband agreed to
watch the children for me so that I could participate, I ignored my
conscience and signed up. The temptation and longing was just
too strong for me to resist. I showed up at the hall on Friday night,
after 'schlepping' all my heavy boxes of photos and accessories
and spread out over the table; but I couldn't get to work on it.
For some reason, my heart just wasn't in it. I kept telling myself,
"This is your chance! This is what you have been waiting for!
What is wrong with you? Just do it!" But I couldn't. I tried.
But there was just no life in it for me. I have come to a place of
knowing when the life of God is in something and when it is just
'dead works'. This thing definitely wasn't breathing. So I went
home early. The next day, I tried again, arriving late, feeling very
uncomfortable and out of place, piddling around until lunch time
– when they served ham sandwiches. Oye. (If you see nothing
wrong with this, go ahead and read my book on Kashrut, Biblical
Dietary Laws.) So I sat down with just some veggies to munch
on and happened to look over at the woman across the table from
me. She wore a T-shirt with a picture of a pig, with some kind of

caption about Canadian Back Bacon. Double oye. Something inside of me said, in a very gentle and loving way, *"Hannah, you do not belong here with these goyim[4] on Shabbat."* I did not sense any accusation or condemnation coming from this voice, and I felt only relief. I left all my things on the table, went home to my family and returned after sundown to pack up.

I tell this story to show you that we all struggle with sometimes wanting to go our own way and do our own pleasure on Shabbat, especially in a world that uses the day for many pleasurable activities. But we are a peculiar people and are called to live a set apart (kadosh) lifestyle that conforms to the ways and commands of God, not the world's. For our obedience, God promises His blessing, and God's blessing is so wonderful; no amount of money can buy His favor on our lives! When we walk in disobedience, we put ourselves under God's curse that nothing can make up for. Blessings and life or curses and death; it is our choice.

The issue of congregational meetings on Shabbat is controversial. We used to attend a congregation on Shabbat morning. I was involved in praise and worship, children's classes, Messianic dance, Hebrew lessons and the bookstore. We had to wake up early, dress and feed all the children, bring enough clothes and snacks and toys and games for them all, rush to get to music practice before the service began, schlepp (haul) all the books back and forth, etc. As you can imagine, by the time I got home to rest on Shabbat afternoon, I was crying out of frustration and exhaustion, knowing that I was being robbed of my Shabbat by going to a congregation to worship God. Now isn't that ridiculous? We tried to talk to the leaders about moving it to the

---

4 Goyim can refer to Gentiles but most often to pagan, heathens, people who do not know God

afternoon, but this suggestion was not received. Here in Israel, it's even worse, since buses don't run on Shabbat and many people don't have cars, so they must hire a taxi (usually an Arab driver) to take them to congregation. Already this is breaking the commandment that everyone, even the stranger amongst us should have a day of rest. Our wanting to go to congregation is making him work on Shabbat.

One Shabbat, we accepted a ride in someone's van to a congregation. We woke up early and schlepped everyone as usual. By the time we got home, I was exhausted, even though I enjoyed the sermon and worship of the meeting. I asked the Lord about this and He showed me this exact scripture. **"Let every man remain in his place; let no man go out of his place on the seventh day**." (Exodus 16:29) No one is to go out from their places on Shabbat. They are to stay home and rest. I don't think this means that we can't go out for a walk; but we are not to go out with the purpose of making a living or anything that can cause stress and aggravation. I am not trying to imply that Shabbat services are a sin, only that perhaps congregational leaders need to consider this issue and perhaps move services to a later time or to havdallah (the service to close Shabbat and commit the following work week to the Lord). For some, the only opportunity to fellowship with other Believers is on a Shabbat service in their area and the exhortation not to give up the assembling of ourselves together is a valid one. It is here that one must follow also the voice of the Holy Spirit. We need the body of Messiah; we need community. I have tried just staying home with my three children in a small apartment for the entire Shabbat and if anyone has found a way to do this and still feel rested by the close, please do let me know! ☺ Some things still must go one; the dog still needs to go for a walk, the kids still need to be fed. If they spill their juice all over the floor, it still needs to be wiped up. But we can do practical things that make for a more restful and holy day, like making sure enough food is cooked the day before (preparation day) so that we only need to warm up leftovers. Shopping and laundry and paperwork can hopefully be completed and if not – well, the sky won't fall down if we just leave it alone for a day. Like my Mom used to say, dirty clothes and dishes don't run away – they wait for us. We can use disposable dishes for a day to give the family dishwasher a break. One of the best things I have found is to invite people over for later in the day to fellowship, eat, sing, and study the parashah (Sabbath scripture portion). Let's not turn Shabbat into a day of isolated, boring misery. I think that in an ideal world, our children would live in safe communities with other Believers where we could turn them loose to play outside, supervised by older children to give us parents a break and a chance to snooze and schmooze[5]. It is my hope and dream to find or create such a safe community of loving disciples of Yeshua where we can 'do life together'. Until then, we must find creative ways of doing Shabbat so that it works for us and our families.

What about all the urgent things that need to be done? For that answer, we can take a cue from His closest followers. After His death, you would think that the women would want to take care of His body immediately and anoint for burial, but instead, they stayed at home and rested according to the commandment.

> **"...And they rested on the Sabbath according to the commandment."** (Luke 23:56)

Now, if the women closest to Yeshua could stay home and rest, even though a task so urgent as anointing the Lord's body for burial lay waiting for them, cannot we also stay home and rest on this one day a week?

---

5 Schmooze – slang for fellowship

A Symbol of Completion & Perfection

It is our great hope and comfort that one day the Messiah will return and will usher in a time of perfect peace and harmony. (Is. 11) There will be no more wars, no sorrow, no sickness or death. No longer will we have to live among the wicked and suffer injustice, persecution, and exploitation.

Shabbat (the number seven) symbolizes completion or perfection. The seventh day in Genesis points to the work of the Messiah and His redemption. Just before the Lord gave up his spirit on the cross, he said, "It is finished". In Hebrew, he said 'nishlam', נשלם which is related to the word 'shalem', שלם which means whole, compete or perfect. Hebrew words are derived from these three letter root (shoresh) words, which gives us so much opportunity to glean an abundance of rich meaning out of a simple word. The word shalem has another meaning and that is 'pay'; l'shalem is to pay for something. And so in that one word, nishlam, Yeshua was saying, "it is finished, completed, made whole and perfect; the entire ransom price for our sins has been paid in full" Halleluyah!   All that needed to be done to achieve our salvation had been accomplished in this once and for all time sacrifice of the Passover lamb – the Lamb of God, the Messiah.

> **"For by one offering He has perfected forever those who are being sanctified**." (Heb. 10:14)

> **"But God demonstrates His own love for us in this: While we were still sinners, Messiah died for us."** (Rom. 5:8)

Just as the blood of the Passover lamb was placed on the

doorposts of the homes of the Israelites in Egypt so that the angel of death would pass over them, all who will believe and receive walk through this doorway of blood into eternal life with God. There is nothing we can do, even through our best efforts to be good, to obtain the righteous standard that God requires to live with Him – that perfect, sinless state is one that only one Man lived – Yeshua the Messiah. The seventh day reminds us that all works are finished, whereas the first day of the week, Sunday, reminds us that there is much work still to be done.

The number seven is the sacred number of the union between God and His creation. Seven symbolizes completion, fullness, wholeness, and perfection. The entirety of human history is to last 7000 years according to Jewish thought. One day is like 1000 years to the Lord. The beginning of the six thousandth (6000th) year is the Sabbath Millennium – one thousand years of perfect Sabbath rest and peace on earth. (Is. 11) We now stand in the Jewish calendar at approximately the year 5796, although a controversy exists over the actual date, and some believe we are much closer to the year 6000 than we think. Let us pray that we will be ready for the day of the Lord's return. The Messianic Age is considered by traditional Judaism, to be a day when, "Hakol yih'ye Shabbat" – all will be Sabbath – rest, peace and joy.

A Call to Holiness

Shabbat reminds us that we are a people sanctified, set apart by the Lord, a chosen people, His special treasure (a segulah).

> **"Now, therefore, if you will indeed obey My voice and keep My covenant, then you shall be a special treasure (segulah) to Me above all people; for all the**

**earth is Mine. And you shall be to Me a kingdom
of priests (mamlechet cohanim) and a holy nation.
(am kadosh) ..."**   (Ex. 19:5-6)

Believers are called to live holy lives. When we honor
Shabbat, we honor God who has sanctified us. Unfortunately,
many Jewish people today, who were called to holiness, do
not keep the Shabbat. We can say the same thing about many
Christians. As people of God, we must separate ourselves from
the ways of the world, of those who do not love and obey God.
It's no wonder that those who are accustomed to living the way
of the world, experience such difficulties when they turn to God
and adjust to living differently than those around them. We are
strangers on this earth, not of this world, but of the heavenly
realm, born of the spirit. This should make a difference in the
way we live our lives – in the way we work, rest, and even in the
way we eat. God has set boundaries to our lives in order to show
us the way to holiness. Here is His word:

**"For you are a holy people to the Lord your God,
and the Lord has chosen you to be a people for
Himself, a special treasure above all the peoples
who are on the face of the earth."** (Deut. 14:2)

Note that this call to holiness is followed by the following
command:

"You shall not eat any detestable thing." [6]
(Deut. 14:3)

---

6 See book, Kashrut, Biblical Dietary Laws, available through our
website:www.voiceforisrael.com or by mail.

It is not only the Jewish people who are called to holiness, and to be a kingdom of priests, but also Gentiles grafted into the nation and covenant through the Jewish Messiah.

> **"But you are a chosen generation, a royal priesthood, (mamlechet cohanim) a holy nation (am kadosh), His own special people, that you may proclaim the praises of Him who called you out of darkness into His marvelous light; who once were not a people but are now the people of God, who had not obtained mercy, but now have obtained mercy."** (1 Pet. 2:9-10)

It is obvious that Peter is not speaking to the Jews here, but to those who were 'once not the people of God', but who have been chosen now through the Messiah's blood. Note, however, that later, Peter exhorts these people to

> **"Have their conduct honorable among the Gentiles."** (1 Pet. 3:12)

The people Peter is addressing, therefore, are no longer considered Gentiles, but a separate people. They are to be careful of their conduct among the Gentiles (heathens) that they continue to live among. Their lives must be different! How? By their conformance to God's commands which the non-believing Gentiles do not obey!

A Holy Bride

To be the "Bride of the Messiah" is to have an intimate relationship with Him. But not all Believers will qualify. Yeshua is returning for a chaste virgin, a spotless bride, without blemish. He cannot marry a Bride defiled by the ways of the world or by rebellion. The word tells us that those who do not walk in the ways of Torah are defiled.

> **"Blessed are the undefiled in the way, who walk in
> the law (Torah) of the Lord."** (Ps. 119:1)

If we choose to walk in rebellion towards the law (Torah) of God, including one of His important commandments – the Sabbath – we disqualify ourselves from ministering to God as the holy priesthood we are meant to be, and potentially bring disaster upon our children.

> **"...Because you have rejected knowledge, I will also
> reject you, that you should be no priest (cohen) to
> Me; seeing that you have forgotten the law (Torah)
> of your God, I will also forget your children."**
> (Hos. 4:6)

This is not a matter of salvation, but of holiness and inheriting God's blessings.

A Matter of the Heart

We must beware of a sand trap, however, that some Sabbath keepers may fall into. Shabbat is not simply a matter of outward compliance to a system of rules and regulations, but a matter of the heart. If we keep Shabbat, but hold hatred in our heart towards a brother or sister, unforgiveness, bitterness, envy or strife, then we are hypocrites and the Lord would rebuke us, just as He did the Pharisees who tithed faithfully, but neglected the more important things – love, justice, and mercy. In a marriage, the partners can begrudgingly keep their obligations to one another and the covenant remains, but it will be a joyless and loveless union. Shabbat is not meant to be the drudgery of obeying a law, but is to be a delight to our souls – time off to spend with God and with one another, to build and re-build relationships, not a legalistic conforming to specific rules.

I recall once, when Shabbat fell on my birthday, and a friend wanted to take me out to eat. I didn't really want to, since I had already been convicted to stay home and rest on Shabbat and keep it holy. But this person, (a non-Sabbath keeper) insisted, and so I gave in. The date was a disaster. We went to a donut shop that was crowded, smoky, and noisy. I got into an argument with my friend and harbored bitterness in my heart against him. The next day, I walked around nursing this resentment, and feeling quite holier-than-thou for defending my right to keep Shabbat, when I heard a small voice inside say, 'You hypocrite!'

Indeed, when Yeshua was asked what is the most important commandment? He answered with two of them – to love God with all our heart, souls, and strength, and also to love our neighbor as ourselves. And so if we are not loving our brother or sister, but rather hating them in our hearts, then we are in danger of the lake of fire, whether we keep Shabbat or not. For Yeshua says that if we do not forgive those who have sinned against us, then our heavenly Father will not forgive us. If we keep Shabbat scrupulously each week, but hate our brother in our heart, then we are still walking in darkness.

> **"He who says he is in the light, and hates his brother**
> **is in darkness until now...he who hates his brother**
> **is in darkness and walks in darkness and does not**
> **know where he is going, because the darkness has**
> **blinded his eyes."** (1 John 2:9-11)

How do we know if we have crossed over from death to life?
Love. We love people. (John 3:14)

CHAPTER TWO

WHY OBSERVE A SEVENTH DAY SHABBAT REST?

1. Out of Obedience - because the Lord blessed it and made it holy.

> **"Remember the Sabbath day by keeping it holy. Six days you shall labor and do all your work, but the seventh day is a Sabbath to the Lord your God. On it you shall not do any work, neither you, nor your son or daughter, nor your manservant or maidservant, nor your animals, nor the alien within your gates. For in six days the Lord made the heavens and the earth, the sea, and all that is in them, but he rested on the seventh day. Therefore the Lord blessed the Sabbath day and made it holy."** (Ex. 20:8-11)

2. To remember that we are no longer slaves to the world and to Satan.

> **"Remember that you were slaves in Egypt and the**

**Lord your God brought you out of there with a
mighty hand and an outstretched arm. Therefore
the Lord your God has commanded you to observe
the Sabbath day."** (Deut. 5:15)

3. Because the Lord made the Sabbath for all mankind.

**"By the seventh day God had finished the work He
had been doing; so on the seventh day He rested
from all His work. And God blessed the seventh
day and made it holy, because on it He rested from
all the work of creating that He had done."**
(Gen. 2:2-3)

**"The Sabbath was made for man, not man for the
Sabbath. So the Son of Man is Lord even of the
Sabbath."** (Mark 2:27-28)

4. Because when God creates the new heaven and new earth,
we will be required to keep the seventh day Shabbat.

**"From one New Moon to another and from one
Sabbath to another, all mankind will come and
bow down before Me.' says the Lord."** (Is. 66:23)

5. Because the Lord did not abolish the Law or the prophets
and whoever breaks the commandments or teaches others to do
so will be the least in the kingdom of heaven.

**"Do not think that I have come to abolish the Law
or the Prophets; I have not come to abolish them
but to fulfill them. I tell you the truth, until heaven
and earth disappear, not the smallest letter, not the**

least stroke of a pen, will by any means disappear from the Law until everything is accomplished. Anyone who breaks one of the least of these commandments and teaches others to do the same will be called least in the kingdom of heaven, but whoever practices and teaches these commands will be called great in the kingdom of heaven." (Matt. 5:17-19)

6.   Because the Lord will reward any Jewish or non-Jewish person who chooses to keep Shabbat with JOY:

"And foreigners who bind themselves to the Lord... and who keep the Sabbath without desecrating it. These I will bring to my holy mountain <u>and give them joy</u> in my house of prayer." (Is. 56:6-7)

"If you keep your feet from breaking the Sabbath and from doing as you please on my holy day, if you call the Sabbath a delight and the Lord's holy day honorable, and if you honor it by not going your own way and not doing as you please or speaking idle words, then you will find your joy in the Lord, and I will cause you to ride on the heights of the land and to feast on the inheritance of your father Jacob." The mouth of the Lord has spoken." (Is. 58:13-14)

7.   Because the Lord has warned us not to take on the ways of the goyim (heathens).

"Do not learn the ways of the heathen nations." (Jer. 10:2)

8. Gentiles in Yeshua have been grafted into the olive tree and become part of the commonwealth of Israel.

> **"If some of the branches have been broken off, and you, though a wild olive shoot, have been grafted in among the others, and now share in the nourishing sap from the olive root, do not boast over those branches. If you do, consider this: you do not support the root, but the root supports you."** (Rom. 11:17-18)

9. God adopts non-Jewish followers of His into His family through the blood of His Son. When someone is adopted into a family, they generally take on the ways of the father who adopted them, and the family they are adopted into.

> **"In love He predestined us to be adopted as His sons through the Messiah Yeshua, in accordance with His pleasure."** (Eph. 1:5)

10. Gentiles in the Messiah are:

> **"No longer foreigners and aliens, but fellow citizens with God's people and members of God's household."** (Eph. 2:19)

11. Following the Messiah means a forsaking of the past and all attachments of paganism, and a pledging of oneself to the one true God and His people.

> **"...Your people shall be my people, and your God my God."** (Ruth 1:16)

12.   The New Covenant, ushered in through the blood of the Messiah at Passover, carries with it the promise that God's commandments in the Torah will become internalized.

> **"...I will put My law in their minds and write it on their hearts. I will be their God, and they will be My people."**   (Jer. 31:33)

13.   Although this new covenant was originally given only to the house of Israel and with the house of Judah, it was extended by God's grace to all of mankind,

> **"It is too small a thing for you to be My servant to restore the tribes of Jacob and bring back those of Israel I have kept. I will also make you light for the Gentiles, that you may bring My salvation (Yeshua) to the ends of the earth."** (Is. 49:6)

14. God warns us not even to worship Him in a pagan, gentile way.

> **"You must not worship the Lord your God in their way."** (Deut. 12:4)

15.   The root of Sunday assembly is the worship of the Sun god on the pagan 'Esteemed Day of the Sun'. God warns His people to come out of paganism, to be separate, sanctified, and holy unto Him.

> **"...Come out of her My people, so that you will not share in her sins, so that you will not receive any of her plagues."** (Rev. 18:4)[1]

---

1 See Come out of Her, Flee Babylon book through our website: www.voiceforisrael.com or by mail.

> **"Therefore come out from them and be separate,
> says the Lord..."** (2 Cor. 6:17)

16. The Lord asks us to obey His commandments and follow in His footsteps. He kept Shabbat.

> **"We know that we have come to know Him if we
> obey His commands. The man who say, 'I know
> Him,' but does not do what He commands is a liar,
> and the truth is not in him...This is how we know
> we are in Him: Whoever claims to live in Him must
> walk as Yeshua did."** (1 John 2:3-6)

17. Yeshua kept the seventh day Sabbath and did not change it. This was a man-made change. Yeshua rebuked the people for following the traditions of men, especially when they contradicted the laws of God.

> **"And why do you break the command of God for
> the sake of your tradition?...They worship Me in
> vain; their teachings are but rules taught by men."**
> (Matt. 15:3,9)

18. If we willfully disobey His commandments, He does not listen to our prayers.

> **"When we turn a deaf ear to the laws and
> commandments of God, even our prayers are
> detestable to Him."** (Prov. 28:9)

19. People who walk according to the law of the Lord are blessed.

"Blessed are they whose ways are blameless, who walk according to the law of the Lord. Blessed are they who keep His statutes and seek Him with all their heart." (Ps. 119:1-2)

20.   God expects His laws to be obeyed.

"You have laid down precepts that are to be fully obeyed." (Ps. 119:4)

21.   God's people are to be holy.

"But just as He who called you is holy, so be holy in all you do; for it is written, 'Be holy, because I am holy.'" (1 Pet. 1:15-16)

"But you are a chosen people, a royal priesthood, a holy nation, a people belonging to God, that you may declare the praises of Him who called you out of darkness into His wonderful light. Once you were not a people, but now you are the people of God; once you had not received mercy, but now you have received mercy." (1 Pet. 2:9-10)

22.   Keeping the Sabbath day holy has no less importance or value than the other nine of the ten commandments against idolatry, murder, adultery, stealing, or lying (Ex. 20:1-17).

23.   Not working on the Sabbath demonstrates our trust in the abundant provision of God. If we work on the Sabbath day, we show God that we don't really think He can provide for us in the other six working days provided.

"...Tomorrow is to be a day of rest, a holy Sabbath
to the Lord. So bake what you want to bake and
boil what you want to boil. Save whatever is left and
keep it until morning...Six days you are to gather
it (manna), but on the seventh day, the Sabbath,
there will not be any...How long will you refuse
to keep My commands and My instructions? Bear
in mind that the Lord has given you the Sabbath;
that is why on the sixth day He gives you bread for
two days. <u>Everyone is to stay where he is on the
seventh day; no one is to go out.' So the people
rested on the seventh day.</u>"   (Ex. 16:23-30)

24.   The seventh day Sabbath is a sign of the covenant between
God and His people. It is a reminder that we are to be holy people for
the Lord.

"Say to the Israelites, 'You must observe My
Sabbaths.' This will be a sign between Me and you
for the generations to come, so you may know that
I am the Lord, who makes you holy." (Ex. 31:13)

"Also I gave them My Sabbaths as a sign between
us, so they would know that I the Lord made them
holy." (Ezek. 20:12)

25. The penalty for desecrating the Sabbath was death.

"Observe the Sabbath, because it is holy to you.
Anyone who desecrates it must be put to death,
whoever does any work on that day must be cut off
from his people...Whoever does any work on the
Sabbath day must be put to death." (Ex. 31:14-15)

> **"While the Israelites were in the desert, a man was found gathering wood on the Sabbath day. Those who found him gathering wood brought him to Moses and Aaron and the whole assembly, and they kept him in custody, because it was not clear what should be done to him. Then the Lord said to Moses, 'The man must die. The whole assembly must stone him outside the camp.' So the assembly took him outside the camp and stoned him to death, as the Lord commanded Moses."** (Num. 15:32-36)

26. The same laws and regulations are to apply to the native born Israelite and to the aliens and foreigners who join Israel.

> **"<u>The same law</u> applies to the native-born and to the alien living among you."** (Ex. 12:49)

> **"The community is to have the same rules for you and for the alien living among you; this is a lasting ordinance for the generations to come. You and the alien shall be the same before the Lord. <u>The same laws and regulations</u> will apply both to you and to the alien living among you."**
> (Num. 15:15-16)

27. The women closest to the Lord rested on the Sabbath.

> **"Then they went home and prepared spices and perfumes. <u>But they rested on the Sabbath in obedience to the commandment.</u>"** (Luke 23:56)

28. Entering God's rest also means resting from our own work, just as God did from His. We are not to follow the example of disobedience of other people who do not rest on the Sabbath day.

> **"There remains, then, a Sabbath-rest for the people of God; for anyone who enters God's rest also rests from his own work, just as God did from His. Let us, therefore make every effort to enter that rest, so that no one will fall by following their example of disobedience."** (Heb. 4:9-11)

29. We cannot arrogantly assume that the 'blood of Jesus' will cover all our willful, deliberate, repetitive sins after the Truth has been revealed to us.

> **"If we deliberately keep sinning (breaking God's commandments) after we have received the knowledge of the truth, no sacrifice for sins is left, but only a fearful expectation of judgment and of raging fire that will consume the enemies of God."** (Heb. 10:26-27)

CHAPTER THREE

A COUNTERFEIT SABBATH SUNDAY: 'THE ESTEEMED DAY OF THE SUN'

Many people assume that 'somewhere along the way', the Lord or His disciples, or someone in authority must have changed the seventh day Sabbath to the 'Lord's Day on the first day of the week, and that this is why the vast majority of the Christian Church meets on Sunday. Rather than accepting traditions of man, we need to look at the written word of God for the truth. Yeshua, all of His disciples, the apostle Paul and all the early believers honored the seventh day Sabbath and preached in the synagogues on Shabbat. How did the day change to Sunday then? For the answer, we need to examine a bit of history. Under the rule of Emperor Hadrian (117-135 AD), the Romans began a period of anti-Jewish oppression and persecution. To avoid coming under the same persecution themselves, the Christian Church began to pull away from its Jewish roots in the Messiah, gradually forgetting them completely until very recently, by a mighty move of God's Spirit, Christians are re-discovering their biblical roots.

Under the Emperor Constantine (325 AD), at the Council of Nicea, Christianity was proclaimed the official religion of Rome. Since the body of believers was predominantly Gentile by this time, and since the seeds of anti-Semitism had already been sown through arrogance and ignorance, this Christianity of Constantine's absorbed many pagan elements of its Gentile population and deliberately disowned all Jewish identity. All the Feasts of the Lord were abolished, punishable by imprisonment or death. Circumcision was forbidden, as was keeping a seventh day Sabbath. Instead, a change was made to hold the 'Sabbath' on the 'Esteemed Day of the Sun' (Sunday), a day that was formerly used to worship the pagan sun god. At this time, Easter (a day set aside to worship the Babylonian Goddess, Eashtar) was substituted for Passover and the Feast of Firstfruits. The Feast of Saturnalia, also a pagan celebration, was turned into Christmas, a day to celebrate the birth of Yeshua, (although he was not born on December 25th at all, but likely during the Feast of Tabernacles).

I once heard a statement that *"The Council of Nicea was not when pagans became Christians, but when Christians became pagans."* Early believers, both Jewish and non-Jewish, kept the commandments and ways of the Lord. Basically, the seventh day Sabbath is the sign of the covenant between ourselves and God. Keeping a Sabbath day on Sunday is the sign of aligning oneself with the Babylonian/Roman/pagan world system from which God is trying to extricate His people.

It is a well-documented fact that the papacy, the Roman Catholic Church, claims responsibility for this ungodly, anti-Biblical change of the Sabbath day.

Q. —Which is the Sabbath day?

A. —Saturday is the Sabbath day.

Q. —Why do we observe Sunday instead of Saturday?

A. —We observe Sunday instead of Saturday because the Catholic Church transferred the solemnity from Saturday to Sunday." [1]

In changing the times of the law of God, the Church is aligning itself with the spirit of the anti-Christ, whom the prophet Daniel prophesied would do exactly this.

"He (the anti-Christ) shall think to change times and law (Torah)." (Dan. 7:25)

The Catholic Church has also changed the Ten Commandments to make room for the idolatrous adoration of images and statues. Who gave the Catholic Church the authority to change God's law? And why would we obey the decrees of the Catholic Church rather than the Word of God? People of God, we need to be aware of any allegiance to the demonic spirit of the anti-Christ. Changing the Sabbath day to a counterfeit Sabbath was a breach made in God's law. By keeping the Sabbath on its divinely appointed day, we help to repair the breach and restore the correct pathway.

"And they that shall be of thee shall build the old waste places: thou shalt raise up the foundations of many generations; and thou shalt be called the repairer of the breach, the restorer of paths to dwell in. If thou turn away thy foot from the Sabbath, from doing thy pleasure on My holy day; and call the Sabbath a delight, the holy of the Lord, honorable, and shalt honor Him, not doing thine own ways, nor finding thine own pleasure, nor speaking thine own words; then shalt thou delight thyself in the

---

1 The Convert's Catechism of Catholic Doctrine, by Peter Geiermann, edition of 1957, pg.50

**Lord; and I will cause thee to ride upon the high
places of the earth, and feed thee with the heritage
of Jacob thy father; for the mouth of the Lord hath
spoken it."** (Is. 58:12-14)

There are many people who believe it does not matter which
day we choose as a Sabbath, but God is very precise as to dates
and times. The Lamb of God was crucified and slain for our sins
on the exact same day and time that the Israelites were sacrificing
their own lambs in remembrance of the Passover. It could not
have happened on just any day. Of course, this is not a salvation
issue, but a matter of one's own conscience and the guidance of
the Holy Spirit. This explanation is only meant to give believers a
historical and biblical perspective to choose for oneself and one's
family by scriptural truth, not by tradition. God's appointed times
are like precious gems in a beautiful watch piece, designed by the
master Creator Himself. Who are we to move the jewels around
the face of the dial? Who gave man the authority to make common
what God has made holy?

A Bride Out of Babylon

God is calling His people to a higher level of maturity and
holiness. Not everyone in the Kingdom of heaven will be at
the same level. (Matt. 5:17-19) We have already spoken of the
Bride of Christ, those who will dwell intimately with the Lord,
as being undefiled and unblemished by the ways of the world,
or rebellion against God's Torah. But I believe that the Spirit of
God is desperately trying to get something through to us, through
the mouths and pens (and computers) of many people in this day
through the account of Isaac's marriage to Rebecca.

1. The Father will choose a Bride for His Son from amongst His own kin.

2. The Bride must be willing to follow the Holy Spirit out of Babylon (false religion).

If we look at the marriage of Isaac and Rebecca, we can see a foreshadowed picture of the marriage of the Bride to her Messiah. The Father, Abraham, represents God the Father. He commissioned his servant, Eliezer, to choose a bride for his son Yitzhak (Isaac). Eliezer's name in Hebrew means helper of my God. Who, in scripture, is called 'The Helper'? Yeshua promised not to leave us orphans but to send a 'Helper' from God, His Holy Spirit. And so, Eliezer represents the Holy Spirit, sent out by God to choose the Bride for His son, Yeshua, represented by Yitzchak. Eliezer was strictly instructed not to choose a bride for Isaac from among the pagans, the Canaanites, but from his own kindred.

> **"But you shall go to my country and to my family,
> and take a wife for my son Isaac."** (Gen. 24:4)

The Bride of Yeshua will also be from among those who are truly grafted into the commonwealth of Israel through the blood of Messiah Yeshua.

> **"Now, therefore, you are no longer strangers and
> foreigners, but fellow citizens with the saints and
> members of the household of God."** (Eph. 2:19)

The Bride will be chosen from people who have declared, like Ruth,

> **"Your people shall be my people and your God my
> God."** (Ruth 1:16)

What of those in the Church who see neither connection nor kinship between themselves and Israel or the Jewish people? Only God knows. The Father will not choose a pagan Canaanite for the holy Bride of His Son. Those who are "in Messiah" are now the seed of Abraham and called his 'kin'. (Gal. 3:29) Rebecca, who represents the Bride, dwelt in Mesopotamia (Babylon) (Gen. 24:10) When asked, she was willing to follow the Father's servant, Eliezer, out of Babylon, into the Promised Land where her bridegroom, the Son, dwelt. It was her choice; she could have refused and chosen to stay where she was comfortable and secure. But she trusted the servant to show her the way; she trusted herself to make the journey through the unknown. She possessed a spirit of adventure and a courage to leave her home and family and to press on to a new chapter of her life. Eliezer knew she was the right one for his master's son because of Rebecca's kind heart towards man and beast and her willingness to go the extra mile. When Eliezer asked for some water, she offered, of her own initiative, to water his camels also. Rebecca was not only kind, adventurous, hard-working and beautiful, but she was also a chaste virgin, living in Baylon. The Father is looking for a virgin Bride without spot or blemish. Many Christians possess the beautiful qualities than indwelt Rebecca (Rivkah) but continue to live in spiritual Babylon. The Church has dwelt in Babylon since it adopted pagan aspects into its religion. The Spirit (helper) is beckoning, inviting, the Bride to come out of Babylon, which represents all false, pagan elements of religion.

> **"And I heard another voice from heaven saying,**
> **'Come out of her, My people, lest you share in her**
> **sins, and lest you receive of her plagues.'"** (Rev. 18:4)

As Gentile Christianity grew and forgot the foundations of its faith, it became an alien religion to the Jewish people who were instructed to keep the ways of Torah and avoid paganism like a plague. Thus a tragic divorce took place between the people of God – His first covenant people, and those grafted (or adopted) into God's family through the blood of the Messiah. The church is not a replacement for Israel; they are joint partakers in the blessings, but also in the responsibilities of being a people chosen by God and set apart for His purposes.

Objections to the Seventh Day Sabbath

Most well-meaning Christians believe that the Sabbath has been changed from Saturday, the seventh day, to Sunday the first, because of the resurrection of Jesus on Sunday. In a recent newsmagazine article, the following statement expressed the commonly held Christian view:

> *"Jewish believers were so sure of Jesus' Messiahship that they discarded their most holy tradition, the Saturday Sabbath, for the Lord's Day, to commemorate His resurrection, which occurred on the first day of the week."* [2]

Notice the perverted implication that the Saturday Sabbath is simply a 'Jewish tradition' rather than a commandment of God. Another Believer here in Israel once told me that she keeps the "Christian Sabbath", not the Jewish Sabbath. How are we ever going to achieve unity if we have two separate days of worship? God clearly states that there is only one standard, one Torah, one law for the people of the God of Abraham. The question is which is the correct day to keep Shabbat? God's word makes the answer clear. It is the seventh day.

---

2   Rev. Max Solbrekken, '*The Jewish People and the Jesus Wave*', Edmonton Senior, May 2001

I will attempt to address some of the common scriptures used to justify a Sunday Sabbath:

Answering Gentile Objections

1. The first Believers held their meetings on the first day of the week.

> **"On the first day of the week we came together to break bread. Paul spoke to the people and, because he intended to leave the next day, kept on talking until midnight...After talking until daylight, he left."** (Acts 20:7, 11)

According to God's word and Jewish custom, the day always begins the evening before. Meeting on the first day of the week was probably Saturday evening which makes more sense, since Paul preached all night. It is unlikely that he preached from early Sunday morning until midnight and then until daylight Monday morning. I've heard of long church services, but... Jewish people commonly meet on Saturday evenings after sundown, called Motzei Shabbat, for a last meal and Havdallah[3] service to end Shabbat.

2. Collections were made on the first day of the week.

> **"On the first day of every week, each one of you should set aside a sum of money in keeping with his income, saving it up, so that when I come no collections will have to be made."** (1 Cor. 16:2)

---

3 Havdallah is a special service to mark the end of the Sabbath and the beginning of the work week, the division of the holy from the secular.

Since the new believers were all zealous for the Torah, **"... You see, brother, how many thousands of Jews have believed, and all of them are zealous for the Torah."** (Acts 21:20) it is unlikely that they would carry out any financial transactions (a prohibited activity) on the Sabbath day when they worshipped. It is likely that they would take up a collection for God's people on the first day of the week, possibly at the Motz'ei-Shabbat (Saturday evening meal and service).

3. The Torah (law) is based on weak, beggarly (miserable) principles and turning to them means backsliding into bondage. We are not to observe these special days or times.

> **"But now that you know God – or rather are known by God – how is it that you are turning back to those weak and miserable principles? Do you wish to be enslaved by them all over again? You are observing special days and months and seasons and years!"** (Gal. 4:9-10)

Paul needed to emphasize to the Galatians that we cannot obtain righteousness with God through our own works and adherence to the Torah, but through the Lord's atonement alone. It is likely that the Galatians Church had become out of balance in this regard, as do some congregations still today. However, if Paul did not believe in keeping a Saturday Sabbath, he would have made it clear that he did not. Instead, he defended himself against accusations that he did not keep the commandments. Paul, himself lived in obedience to the Torah (law):

> **"They have been informed that you teach all the Jews who live among the Gentiles to turn away from Moses, telling them not to circumcise their children or live according to our customs...Take**

> these men, join in their purification rites and pay
> their expenses, so that they can have their heads
> shaved. Then everybody will know <u>there is no truth
> in these reports about you, but that you yourself
> are living in obedience to the Torah (law).</u>" (Acts
> 21:21-24)

4. Christians should worship on Sundays to honor the Lord's resurrection.

Paul preached on the seventh day Sabbath, not on Sundays.

> "On the next Sabbath almost the whole city came
> together to hear the word of God." (Acts 13:44)

<u>There was no special Sunday meeting for the Greeks or
Gentiles; they met together.</u>

> "And he reasoned in the synagogue every Sabbath,
> and persuaded both Jews and Greeks." (Acts
> 18:4)

Yeshua's custom was to go to synagogue on the Sabbath to read from the Torah.

> "Then Yeshua returned in the power of the Spirit
> to Galilee, and news of Him went out through all
> the surrounding region. And He taught in their
> synagogues, being glorified by all. So He came to
> Nazareth, where He had been brought up. <u>And as
> His custom was, He went into the synagogue on the
> Sabbath day,</u> and stood up to read." (Luke 4:14-16)

In answer to this specific objection about not observing special days and times, we could ask, "If we are not to observe special days, then why do Christians celebrate Christmas and Easter, which are both unscriptural celebrations?"

5. Sunday is The Lord's day

> **"On the Lord's day I was in the Spirit.."** (Rev.
> 1:10)

Why do Christians assume that 'the Lord's day' means Sunday? Yeshua himself said that He is Lord of the Sabbath.

> **"So the Son of Man is Lord even of the Sabbath."**
> (Mark 2:28)

If this is true, then wouldn't the Sabbath more likely be 'The Lord's Day'?

Another reference to 'The Lord's Day' is the great and terrible day of judgment, which is coming upon the earth.

> **"Blow the trumpet in Zion; sound the alarm on My
> holy hill. Let all who live in the land tremble, for
> the day of the Lord is coming."** (Joel 2:1)

The day of the Lord here is not Sunday but the time of Yeshua's second coming.

6. Sunday is the resurrection day.

> **"After the Sabbath, at dawn on the first day of the
> week, Miryam of Magdala and the other Miryam
> went to look at the tomb."** (Matt.28:1)

The majority of the Christian church assumes Sunday to be the day of the Lord's resurrection, and they therefore justify a Sunday meeting for worship, prayer, and preaching. There is nothing wrong with meeting to worship the Lord together on Sunday, just as it is acceptable to worship the Lord every day of the week, as long as it is clear that the Sabbath day of rest is still Saturday, the seventh day. The Lord was likely resurrected on motzei Shabbat (Saturday evening).

Notice that at dawn on the first day of the week (Sunday), the tomb was already empty.

> **"He is not here; He has risen, just as He said."**
> (Matt. 28:6)

This is because, according to the Lord's own words, He would rise exactly three days and three nights after being placed in the tomb. This was the sign of Jonah he spoke of.

> **"For as Jonah was three days and three nights in the belly of a huge fish, so the Son of Man will be three days and three nights in the heart of the earth."** (Matt. 12:40)

If these words are not true, then Yeshua is not a true prophet, but a liar. If we count from 'Good Friday' until 'Easter Sunday', we certainly cannot count three days and three nights. In fact, Yeshua was crucified as the Passover lamb on the day of Passover to fulfill scriptures perfectly. This was Wednesday, the day of preparation (the day before the Sabbath) (Mark 15:42), (John 19:42). But this was not the regular seventh day Sabbath which was approaching as they hurried to get Him down off the cross, but the High Sabbath which is the first day of the Feast of Unleavened bread, a holy day on which no work is to be done.

> **"On the first day hold a sacred assembly and do no regular work."** (Lev. 23:7)

The first and last days of Passover are Sabbaths no matter what day of the week they happen to fall on in that particular year. Sometimes they fall on a seventh day Sabbath but other times they do not. People sometimes confuse the timing of the death and resurrection of Yeshua because of this misunderstanding. In fact, Yeshua was resurrected on motzei Shabbat and offered to the Father as the first fruits on – guess what? The Feast of First Fruits! This feast occurred three days after the Passover day, and was the time when the cohen (priest) would offer the first fruits of the barley crop up to the Father as an offering. This is why Yeshua said to Miryam,

> **"Do not hold on to Me, for I have not yet returned to the Father."** (John 20:17)

He had not yet been offered up to the Father as the first fruits offering. The barley represented the first sign of life after the death of winter. Yeshua represents the first to be raised from the dead, and is the promise to us that we will follow Him.

> **"But the Messiah has indeed been raised from the dead, the first fruits of those who have fallen asleep. For since death came through a man, the resurrection of the dead comes also through a man. For as in Adam all die, so in the Messiah all will be made alive. But each in his own turn: Messiah, the first fruits; then, when He comes, those who belong to Him."** (1 Cor. 15:20-23)

7. The Jerusalem Council.

> **"It is my judgment, therefore that we should not make it difficult for the Gentiles, who are turning to God. Instead we should write to them telling them to abstain from food polluted by idols, from sexual immorality, from the meat of strangled animals and from blood. <u>For Moses has been preached in every city from the earliest times and is read in the synagogues on every Sabbath.</u>"** (Acts 15:19-21)

This scripture has been used by non-Jewish believers to justify their not keeping the commandments of God. First of all, these Gentiles they are referring to here are pagan, heathen people, idolaters who know nothing about God, but are just turning to Him. They are not the same as 'Gentile Believers' who have God's word as their guide.

Secondly, although these few stipulations are a starting point, notice that the scriptures mention Moses being preached in the synagogues every Sabbath, where the new Believers ('Followers of the Way'), would be expected to go to worship God and be discipled in His ways. Gentiles were never given a free ticket to live in whatever way they choose and disobey God's commandments.

> **"For sin shall not be your master, because you are not under law, but under grace. What then? Shall we sin because we are not under law but under grace? By no means!...You have been set free from sin and have become slaves to righteousness."** (Rom. 6:14-18)

People who did not formerly know God were expected to gradually move in the direction of a Torah-obedient, God-pleasing lifestyle, and forsake all pagan customs.

Thirdly, notice that Gentiles are not specifically forbidden from murder, theft, dishonoring of parents, or covetousness. Does this mean that Gentiles are allowed to commit these sins because **"...it seemed good to the Holy Spirit and to us not to burden you with anything beyond the following requirements."** (Acts 15:28) Of course not! The Ten Commandments, which include keeping the Sabbath day holy, are basic moral laws that all people, both Jew and Gentile, are simply expected to obey for their own good.[4] While most Christians would never seriously consider breaking the other commandments, many treat the on the Sabbath commandment as a frivolous suggestion, not nearly as serious as the law on tithing!

Did God change His mind about Shabbat?

> **"For I am the Lord God, I do not change."** (Mal. 3:6)

Did the Messiah change His mind about Shabbat?

> **"Yeshua the Messiah is the same yesterday, today and forever."** (Heb. 13:8)

Could God and His Messiah disagree about the day of the Sabbath rest?

> **"Hear O Israel, the Lord our God, the Lord is One."** (Deut. 6:4)

---

4 Many people believe that Gentiles are only required to keep what is referred to as the 'Noachide Laws' - seven minimun commandments for all humankind given 'supposably' to Noah. This is not biblical truth but oral tradition only.

CHAPTER FOUR

OTHER BENEFITS OF KEEPING THE SABBATH

1.   It breaks the cycle of 'busyness' in our lives.

2.   It breaks the bondage of workaholism.

3.   It gives a rhythm and cycle to our week.

4.   It gives us time to read, relax, and other things we never have time for.

5.   It gives us a break from chauffeuring our kids all over town.

6.   It gives us a break from the cares and concerns of everyday life.

7.   It keeps 'the world' out for one day a week, and gives God room to enter.

8.   It gives us quality, unhurried time to spend with our loved ones, to build and re-build intimate relationships.

9. It gives women a day off as well – no laundry, cooking or dishes - leftovers on paper plates and close the laundry room door if sundown came before the laundry was done.

10. It gives a set day before Shabbat to get the house cleaned and in order.

11. It gives one evening in the week to eat a full, healthy, leisurely meal with all family members present, and to talk together.

12. For one day a week, you can stay home. You have nowhere you have to rush off to.

13. You get a break -You don't have to dress up, wear pantyhose, makeup, or shave!

14. When you slow down enough, you may realize how weary you really are.

15. It breaks the Martha syndrome and transforms us into Mary's.

16. We can be totally useless one day a week, and still know we are loved and accepted by God and by others. It breaks our striving for acceptance by 'achievement'.

17. It gives us a specific time to bless our children.

18. We can enjoy a little glass of Sweet "Kiddush" (Sanctified) wine.

19. Candles are romantic.

20. We have an excuse to unplug the phone, sleep in, and nap in the afternoon without being accused of laziness.

21. Families can turn away from their electronic world of computers, iPods, televisions, video games and instead relate to God and to one another. Be still and know that I am God.

CHAPTER FIVE

HOW TO CELEBRATE THE SABBATH

The question that arises in how to celebrate the Sabbath is what constitutes work and rest? The word used in Scripture is not actually against work, which would be 'avodah' but 'm'lachah', which means 'vocation'. One person's pleasure is another person's toil. For example, a person who earns his living fishing would not find it restful to go fishing, but another person might call fishing very restful. A professional chef would be working if he was cooking on his day off, but someone else might enjoy tending a barbeque on his or her day off.[1]

Another question is how to keep Shabbat holy. We have already touched on this subject by clarifying Shabbat as a holy day of rest, not a day for recreational activities. But Scripture is not black and white on this subject; there is much room for grey areas which means we must seek for wisdom from the Holy Spirit. Also, modern life has made for many issues that Moses didn't have to deal with: microwaves, telephones, electricity, cars, etc.

---

1 The Hebrew word used in Exodus 20:10 is not avodah (work) but rather M'lachah (vocation). We are not to practice our vocation on Shabbat, even if we enjoy it or are behind running schedule.

To eliminate these grey areas, modern Rabbinical Judaism has 39 categories of forbidden acts. The prohibition against lighting a fire has raised some controversy. What about using electricity? Many Jewish people will not turn on a light switch on Shabbat. What about lighting a gas stove? Can you heat up food on Shabbat in the microwave? What about the fire of internal combustion of an engine – can we drive on Shabbat? Shabbat was never meant to be an exercise in legalism, a precise list of do's and don'ts. Orthodox Rabbinical Judaism has taken this to an extreme, and has regulated exactly what one may and may not do on the Sabbath.

According to the Shulchan Aruch, (A Prepared Table) the compilation and codification of instructions regarding Jewish ritual observances, written by Joseph Karo (with the help of his 'spirit guide') here are some of the rules:

> *"You should not climb trees on the Sabbath. Nor should you swing from a tree limb. You could spit, provided you did not rub the spit into the ground with your toe- but you could step on the spit as long as you kept your foot still. Umbrellas were forbidden- opening one would be like erecting a "tent". Fingers should not be snapped. NO musical instruments should be played. If a fire broke out – what could one do? It was forbidden to extinguish a fire on the Sabbath. And it was also forbidden to 'carry' things. Ergo- it was ruled that in case of a house on fire, nothing should be saved...watches should not be carried on the Sabbath. Keys might be carried, so long as it appeared that they were only jewelry... Similarly, handkerchiefs could not be carried in the pocket; but they could be tied about the sleeve*

or leg, so as to seem a part of the clothing... " [2]

Are you starting to get the picture? No wonder so many Jewish people become disillusioned with Orthodox Rabbinical Judaism, which is for most the only way they know of to live in obedience to God. In a reaction against this kind of legalism and strict adherence to man-made rules, many Jewish people 'throw out the baby with the bath water' and reject God completely, thinking that He was the one demanding compliance with this kind of shtuyot (nonsense). Members of my own family would not re-light the pilot light on the furnace when it went out one cold, winter day in Canada. And so they sat inside wearing winter coats all Shabbat, the baby's lips turning blue, rather than call in a service man to light the fire in the furnace on Shabbat. We need to use some common sense. I don't believe that this is in the spirit of Shabbat. Well meaning people who think that to please God they must observe Sabbath according to these Rabbinic standards should know that traditional Judaism of today is not the form of religion of Moses and the prophets. It is a man-made religion of rabbis who lived and taught their rules 1500 years later. It is a religion based more on the Talmud (oral law) than the Torah (Bible). The traditional Judaism of our day has its roots in the religion of the Pharisees, a small group of Jews who banded together over two thousand years ago.[3] They were famous for their attention to detail – they would not eat with ceremonially unwashed hands. They are why today, in most religious Jewish homes and Orthodox synagogues, one cannot even rip off a piece of toilet paper on Shabbat – they have to be pre-ripped before Shabbat. Yes, I am totally serious. Why am

---

2 Richard Chaimberlin's publication, '*Petach Tikvah*' (Door of Hope) contains an excellent article in its Jan-March 2001 issue, pg. 16, by Randolph Parrish, '*The Mother of All Books*' (165 Rochester Road, Rochester, NY 14623)

3 Yeshua, Who Is He? By Dr. Michael L. Brown, Messianic Vision, Inc.

I coming down so hard on people adhering to Rabbinic Judaism of today? It is because I have seen way too many sincere, Christian people turn to Torah and Rabbinic Judaism and the synagogue and leave Yeshua behind in the dust.[4] Traditional Judaism as we know it today is a reaction against Yeshua; it is a religion of those who hate and reject Yeshua. It is a system which has been reconstructed to negate every legitimate claim that Yeshua is the Messiah. When we lived in Israel and came out from our Messianic congregation in Jerusalem, anti-Missionaries were there handing out pamphlets that read, "10 reasons why beer is better than Jesus." Children are indoctrinated into this system at an early age. Sometimes we would go to the playground on Shabbat where Israeli children were playing. They would point fingers and tell us we were breaking Shabbat if my kids began to dig and play in the sand. Of course there is nothing in the Torah to support their beliefs; these are all rules made up by various rabbis. Sometimes even Messianic Jews begin to live like this. We visited one family in Israel who live as Orthodox Jews and sent their children to religious schools for their education. One Shabbat, we went out into the yard and I noticed the pet turtles' bowl of water had overturned. I was about to refill it but their little girl stopped me, saying that I might break Shabbat if the grass was inadvertently watered. Oye. It was exactly this kind of legalism that caused me to turn away from God and my family and begin to seek for spiritual truths in Eastern religions, mysticism and occult. If we could understand that God's heart is for a relationship with us, and that Yeshua is the way to the Father, it would totally transform our lives and our motivation for keeping God's commandments, including that of observing a Shabbat day.

As a woman with small children, I have often struggled with

---

4 Please read article Falling Away in articles archives on our website:www. voiceforisrael.com

how to receive a day of rest while still changing diapers and caring for my family. God does love women, however, as well as men, and He wants us also to have a day off from cooking and laundry and washing pots and pans as well. We may cook enough food on Friday to last us for Shabbat day and eat cold leftovers without having to cook or light a fire. Personally, we even go so far as to eat on paper plates on Shabbat so that we are not left with a big stack of dishes Saturday night. Some people don't mind washing dishes! Every family can find ways to keep Shabbat a day of rest for each one in the family, without it disintegrating into a joyless, legalistic, heavy burden that it was never meant to be. We must use common sense, and observe the Shabbat in the spirit of the law and with a right heart attitude, keeping in mind that defiling the Sabbath was a major sin, resulting in the destruction of the temple and sending God's people into exile. Transgressing the Sabbath resulted in a death penalty. Even though Yeshua has taken the penalty for our sins, we are still to obey God's commandments out of love and respect for Him.

I have outlined some scriptural and traditional guidelines for celebrating Shabbat, but each home will have to establish their own specific boundaries to keep the peace and rest of Shabbat. It is important to follow the leading of the Holy Spirit and remember that the Lord always looks upon the heart first and foremost.

Celebrate Shabbat:

1.   In a spirit of joy and delight, not legalism.

2.   With a right heart attitude – not outward compliance to the commandment with darkness hidden in our hearts.

3.   Refrain from vocational work and trust God to supply all our needs in six days given to labor. I believe that this applies even

if one enjoys their work; it is still their vocation.

4. Follow Yeshua's example: do good, tend to your own human needs, minister healing and life to others, worship and honor God and study His Word; teach it to your children.

5. Prepare your home in advance – clean, shop, and finish laundry; bake or buy Challah (special Sabbath bread); wine (or grape juice), candles; have enough food prepared for next day, so you don't have to cook on Shabbat.

6. Start on Friday evening with blessing the Challah and wine, enjoying a special, unhurried family meal, lighting the candles at sundown. Husbands can bless their wives and parents bless their children.[5]

7. Seek the Lord and the guidance of the Holy Spirit as a family (couple, single) to re-order
priorities so that the Sabbath day may be kept holy.

8. Activities to avoid may include working, travelling, cooking, economic transactions (shopping), 'schlepping' (carrying), creating or 'doing'. Each person must search their own conscience for what constitutes work and contributes to their stress, and what is restful; what is holy and what is profane. Let peace and the Word of God be your judge. Remember that although God rested on the Shabbat, the sun still rose and set. Some basic activities must carry on i.e. childcare.

9. Finding rest for our souls. Equally as important as physical rest is spiritual rest. On Shabbat, we remember that the Messiah

5 These are all traditions, not commandments.

completed all that needed to be done for our eternal salvation and to reconcile us in peace with God. The Lord's last recorded words were, '**...It is finished'. Then He bowed His head and gave up His spirit.**" (John 19:30)
So we too must remind ourselves that 'It is finished'. We can rest in what He has done. Our physical rest from work is a physical reminder of the spiritual rest we have in the Lord.

> **"Come unto Me, all you who are weary and heavy laden and I will give you rest. Take My yoke upon you and learn from Me, for I am gentle and humble in heart, and you will find rest for your souls. For My yoke is easy and My burden is light."** (Matt. 11:28-30)

The seventh day represents all the work being finished. The first day of the week represents much left to be done.

10. Fellowship with believers, reach out to sinners as Yeshua did, play with your kids, go for walks in nature, hold hands, hug, watch flowers grow, read, watch an edifying video, or listen to a tape, take a nap, make love with your spouse, read the weekly Sabbath portion (parashah)[6] and discuss it with friends over leftover lunch and leisurely tea. As much as possible, turn off the electronics and play board games or find some way to relate to one another and to God.

---

6 Messianic Jewish commentary on parashot available on our website www. voiceforisrael.com.

CHAPTER SIX

CONCLUSION: A PROPHETIC VIEW OF SHABBAT

Our study of Shabbat would be incomplete without a discussion of the prophetic view of this special day. The great hope of Jewish people, and in fact all people of the God of Abraham, is that of the Messianic Age, followed by a time of universal harmony. It will begin a time of perfect peace, joy, and happiness, ending all war, injustice and exploitation. The Messianic Age is called in Hebrew *Yom Shekulo Shabbat* - the day when all will be Sabbath. (Kaplan, Aryeh, Sabbath, Day of Eternity). Thus, the Sabbath is a preparation or dress rehearsal for the time when our Messiah will dwell with us (Immanu-El – God with us).

> **"And I heard a loud voice from heaven, saying, "Behold, the tabernacle of God is with men, and He will dwell with them, and they shall be His people. God Himself will be with them and be their God. And God will wipe away every tear from their eyes; there shall be no more death, nor sorrow, nor crying. There shall be no more pain, for the former things have passed away."** (Rev. 21:3-4)

Of this time, the prophet Isaiah tells us,

> **"He will swallow up death forever, and the Lord**
> **God will wipe away tears from all faces."**
> (Is. 25:8)

This is something that we need to cling to – the hope that one day God will personally wipe away every tear from our eyes. On Shabbat, we indulge in a taste of this Messianic Kingdom. It is therefore a sin to sorrow or to fast on Shabbat. We must eat, drink and enjoy this life and all the blessings the good Lord has bestowed upon us in His abundant mercy. I believe that this is why breaking Shabbat carried the death penalty. Not that it was so much worse than the other sins, but it proved that the people who would not honor this day could never comprehend the Messianic Day that is promised to await those of us who wait for Him.

Who will have a right to the tree of life and to enter the gates into the city (The New Jerusalem)? **"Those who do His commandments."** (Rev. 22:14)

Awesome words. Anyone who loves and practices a lie will not enter the kingdom but will remain outside where there will be weeping and gnashing of teeth. Even some in deliverance and healing ministries will be cast out, according to the Lord's own words.

> **"Not everyone who says to Me, 'Lord, Lord,' shall**
> **enter the kingdom of heaven, but he who does the**
> **will of My Father in heaven. Many will say to Me**
> **in that day, 'Lord, Lord, have we not prophesied**
> **in Your name, cast out demons in Your name, and**
> **done many wonders in Your name?' And then I**

> **will declare to them, 'I never knew you; <u>depart</u>**
> **<u>from Me, you who practice lawlessness!'"</u>**
> (Matt. 7:21-23)

Why? Because they practice lawlessness. Not that they occasionally miss the mark and sin, but they practice the breaking of God's law on a regular basis. If we now know that God has ordained Shabbat on the seventh day as a holy day of rest, according to His command and we instead love and practice the lie that it is changed to Sunday (or worse yet, that it has been abolished completely), then we are continuing in willful sin for which the Word of God says there is no sacrifice. (Heb. 10:26)

God does not hear the prayers of people who knowingly commit deliberate sins. He considers the prayers of those who ignore His Torah as abominable.

> **"He that turns his ear away from hearing the law**
> **(Torah), even his prayer is an abomination."** (Prov.
> 28:9)

We must keep in mind that God wrote the Ten Commandments, including that of keeping Shabbat, on tablets of stone with His very own finger.

> **"And the Lord spoke to you out of the midst of**
> **the fire.... So He declared to you His covenant**
> **which He commanded you to perform, the Ten**
> **Commandments; and He wrote them on two tablets**
> **of stone."** (Deut. 4:12-13)

With the New Covenant, He wrote these commands in our minds and upon our hearts. (Jer.31:31-34) What is the conclusion of the whole matter?

> **"Let us hear the conclusion of the whole matter:
> fear God, and keep His commandments, for this is
> the whole duty of man."** (Eccl. 12:13)

The Fourth commandment tells us to 'Remember the Sabbath'. Why did God tell us to remember? Because He must have known we would forget!

Remember....

APPENDIX

Shabbat blessing over candles[1]

Blessed are You, O Lord our God, King of the Universe...

Baruch ata Adonay Eloheynu melech ha olam...

...who has sanctified us with the blood of Yeshua the Messiah and in whose name we light the Sabbath candles.

...Asher kidshanu b'dam Yeshua ha Mashiach u'bishmo anu madlikim neirot shel Shabbat...

or (alternative)

...who has sanctified us with the blood of Yeshua the Messiah and has commanded us to be a light unto the nations.

...asher kidshanu b'dam Yeshua ha Masshiach v'tzivanu lihyot or l'goyim...

or (alternative)

...who has given us Yeshua the Messiah, the Light of the world and the glory of your people Israel.

---

1 Addapted for followers of Yeshua from traditional Jewish blessing which states that we are sanctified by His commandments and commanded to light the Sabbath candles. This is not Biblically accurate but part of the oral tradition.

...asher natan lanu et Yeshua ha Masshiach, or ha-olam v'kavod am Yisrael.

Note: Appropriate scriptures may be read such as:
"I am the light of the world." (John 8:12)

Sabbath blessing over wine (kiddush)

Blessed are You, O Lord our God King of the Universe who has created the fruit of the vine.

Baruch ata Adonay Eloheynu melech ha olam borey pri ha gafen.

Yeshua held up the cup of wine at the Passover meal and said, "This is the blood of the New Covenant which is shed for many." (Mark 14:23-24)

Blessing over challah (Sabbath bread)

Blessed are You, O Lord our God, King of the Universe, who gives us bread that comes out of the earth.

Baruch ata Adonay Eloheynu melech ha olam, ha motzi lechem min ha aretz.

Yeshua said, **"I am the bread of life. He who comes to Me shall never hunger, and he who believes in Me shall never thirst."** (John 6:35)

BIBLIOGRAPHY

Kaplan, Aryeh, '*Sabbath, Day of Eternity*'.

'*The Sabbath Rest. Saturday Sabbath or the Esteemed Day of the Sun*', First Fruits of Zion, Inc. 1995.

Muller, Wayne, '*Sabbath: Remembering the Sacred Rhythm of Rest and Delight*', 1999.

Howard, Sanford R., '*L'Chayim, Finding the Light of Shalom, What the Rabbis Never Told You!*', 1995-1999.

Chumney, Eddie, '*Who is the Bride of Christ?*' Serenity books, P.O. Box 3595 Hagerstown, MD 21742-3595, 1997.

Chaimberlin, Richard, '*The Mother of all Books*', Petach Tikvah (Door of Hope), Jan-March 2001, Vol. 19, No.1.

To contact the Author write:

Hannah Nesher, Voice for Israel
Suite #313- 11215 Jasper Ave.
Edmonton, Alberta
T5K 0L5 Canada

www.voiceforisrael.net

*Please include your testimony or help received
from this book when you write.*

Your prayer requests are welcome

Additional Teaching Materials by Hannah Nesher

DVDs

Shalom Morah I (Hebrew for Christians &
Hebrew Names of God) 11 DVD set
Shalom Morah II (Hebrew for Christians &
Wisdom in the Hebrew Alphabet) 10 DVD set
Exploring the Jewish Roots of the Christian Faith
Unity in the Messiah
Because He Lives
Messianic Jewish Wedding in Jerusalem
There is a God in Israel
Messianic Jewish Passover
Passover Lamb or Easter Ham?
Voice Out of Zion II (Where is Your Brother Jacob?)
Walking Through the Wilderness
Ruth: A Righteous Gentile
Messiah in Chanukah

BOOKS

Grafted in Again
Journey to Jerusalem
Come Out of Her My People
Messiah Revealed in Purim
Messiah Revealed in Passover
Messiah Revealed in the Fall Feasts
Messiah Revealed in Chanukah
Kashrut: The Biblical Dietary Laws
Messiah Revealed in Shavuot
You Know My Heart (English booklet)
You Know My Heart (Hebrew booklet)